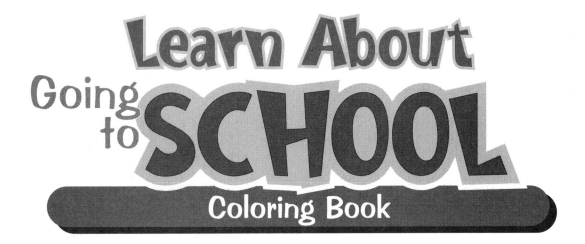

Learn About Going to SCHOOL
Coloring Book

Written by Kaori Crutcher
Illustrated by C.A. Nobens

FS144006 Learn About Going to School
All rights reserved. Printed in the U.S.A.
Copyright © 1999 Frank Schaffer Publications, Inc.
23740 Hawthorne Blvd., Torrance, CA 90505

Name _____

School

School is a place for learning.

3
reproducible

FS144006 Learn About Going to School

Friends

You can make lots of new friends at school.

FS144006 Learn About Going to School

Shapes

Shapes can be found all over school.

13
reproducible

Lots to Learn

You will learn to color, paste, and cut with scissors.

14
reproducible

Name _____

Animals

You will learn about all kinds of animals.

Name _____

People

You will learn about people all over the world.

FS144006 Learn About Going to School

What You Will Be

You will learn about what you want to be when you grow up.

17

reproducible

Name _____

Art Class

Children learn to draw and paint in art class.

18

reproducible

FS144006 Learn About Going to School

Make Things

You may make things at school to bring home.

Music

You may learn to play a musical instrument.

20

Class Pet

Often children raise a class pet.

21
reproducible

Lunch

Children eat lunch with their friends in the cafeteria.

22
reproducible

FS144006 Learn About Going to School

Name _____

Playground

During recess you go out to the playground to run and play.

23

FS144006 Learn About Going to School

Games

On the playground you will play many games.

Seesaw and Swings

The playground is lots of fun.

FS144006 Learn About Going to School

Sandbox

You can also play in a sandbox.

Playroom

Some schools have a playroom to play in.

Name _____

Field Trips

Sometimes the class goes on field trips to interesting places.

reproducible

FS144006 Learn About Going to School

Name _____

Computers

Some schools have computers for students to use.

FS144006 Learn About Going to School

Name _____

School Bus

A school bus brings children to school and takes them home.

FS144006 Learn About Going to School

Name _____

Crossing Guard

A crossing guard helps you get to and from school safely.

FS144006 Learn About Going to School

Learning Is Fun

SCHOOL

Using what you learn at school can be lots of fun.

FS144006 Learn About Going to School